Paul

One Man's Extraordinary Adventures

Ethel Barrett

Regal
Books

A Division of G/L Publications
Ventura, CA U.S.A.

Other good reading in this series:
Elijah and Elisha by Ethel Barrett
Joshua by Ethel Barrett
Joseph by Ethel Barrett
Daniel by Ethel Barrett
Ruth by Ethel Barrett
Birth of the King by Alice Schrage
The King Who Lives Forever by Alice Schrage

The foreign language publishing of all Regal books is under the direction of Gospel Literature International (GLINT). GLINT provides financial and technical help for the adaptation, translation and publishing of books for millions of people worldwide. For more information regarding translation, contact: GLINT, P.O. Box 6688, Ventura, California 93006.

Scripture quotations in this publication are from the *Authorized King James* version.

Published by Regal Books
A Division of GL Publications
Ventura, California 93006.
Printed in U.S.A.

Library of Congress Catalog Card No. 81-51740
ISBN 0-8307-0767-0
RL: 5,6

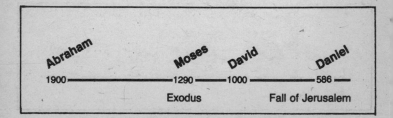

Abraham — 1900 ——— Moses — 1290 ——— David — 1000 ——— Daniel — 586 —

Exodus   Fall of Jerusalem

CONTENTS

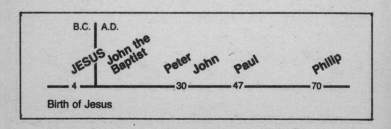

About the Author

Ethel Barrett is one of North America's favorite writers and Bible storytellers. She is the author of over forty books, including seven in this popular Bible Biography series for kids. Her *Stories to Grow On* series was nominated for a Gold Medallion Award in 1979, and her recording of *Ethel Barrett Tells Favorite Bible Stories* was nominated for a Grammy Award in 1978. Ethel Barrett's books are available in bookstores everywhere.

1

PORTRAIT OF
AN EGGHEAD

His name was Saul. And some of his friends may have called him "Egghead" behind his back. He may have been the brightest boy in class, but it's a pretty good guess he may not have been the most popular.

Take games, for instance. They had foot races and tugs-of-war. And contests—like shooting arrows straight and using slingshots properly. We do not know for sure, but it would be a pretty good guess that Saul spent more time studying than he did playing games.

"They call me 'Egghead,' " he said to his father one morning at breakfast. "And what's more, I don't care."

"Egghead indeed," his father snorted.

"That's good. That's a compliment. It's a good thing to be called an egghead. It means you're smart."

"But Saul should be taught other things too," his mother started to say.

"Like what?" his father grunted, reaching for some more barley cakes.

"Things like tenderness," his mother said.

"Bah!" his father said.

"And sympathy and understanding."

"Humbug," his father said as Paul passed him the honey and he slapped it on his barley cakes. "The most important thing in life for Saul to be is—*important*," his father finished.

And that seemed to end the matter, for when Saul's father spoke, that was it. It was very seldom that anyone argued with him. Since no one did, he went on talking, munching his barley cakes all the while. "The important thing in life is to be important, and Saul is going to be important—one of the most important men in the world," he munched. "And the biggest and the brightest," he crunched. "And the one who loves God the most," he gulped.

Now, someone should have thought at this point to tell Saul's father that he shouldn't talk so much with his mouth full, but nobody dared. Instead, Saul said, "I do love God, Father, more than anyone else in the world. I always shall."

"And you're going to keep on loving Him!" his father bellowed. "You will not only love Him but you will uphold His ways and you will know His laws by heart, every single one of them, down to the last period. You will know every law of God so well, my son, that you will be able to unroll one of your books and point to the very page, the very word, without missing a beat. Do you understand?"

"Yes, Father," Saul said.

Any talk of sympathy or tenderness or kindness was forgotten. When Father said something, that was *that*.

The meal was finished; Saul washed his face and hands, rolled up the book he was studying for the day, kissed his father and mother good-bye and scampered off to school.

He joined his friends as they scrambled out of their houses one by one, all freshly

scrubbed, with their copybooks rolled under
their arms. They were going to the synagogue
where their teachers would teach them more of
the Word of God for almost the rest of the
day.

There was no doubt that Saul was the
smartest boy in the class. There was not one
law of God that he could not put his fingers on
and quote from memory before any of the
other kids hardly had a chance to raise their
hands. It wasn't that the other boys were
dumb—far from it. It was just that Saul was
just a little bit *smarter* than most of the others
and he jolly well knew it and was proud of it.

But being proud of just being a good
student was hardly enough for a boy like Saul.
No indeed. When he wasn't busy studying at
school or studying at home by the light of the
oil lamp in the corner of his father's house, or
studying in the library, he squeezed in time
getting to know the games of skill.

Nobody knew the rules of the footrace any
better than Saul did. Nobody knew how
important it was to shoot an arrow straight or
to swing a sling or send a stone in a perfect

line to hit its mark. Nobody knew the rules of
running and wrestling better than Saul did. So
Saul had that to be proud of too.

And as if that were not enough, Saul could
be proud of where he lived.

Tarsus!

Now Tarsus was no ordinary little country
town where a sign said "WELCOME TO
TARSUS," and another sign a mile down the
road said "FAREWELL TO TARSUS," before
you could hardly blink. No siree. If you
wanted to walk around Tarsus you had many,
many miles to go and many, many fascinating
sights to see, for more than half-a-million
people lived there. Some of the greatest stores
and trading centers were located there. Why,
the River Cydnus was a great river port; ships
from all over the world stopped there and
bought and sold, and traded their goods.

There wasn't a day went by that the
caravans did not stream back and forth, to and
from the ships, loading and unloading.
Anything in the world you wanted to buy, you
could buy in Tarsus. Any gossip in the world
you wanted to hear you could hear in Tarsus,

if you kept your ears open. Now all of this would be quite enough to boggle the mind of any boy, but believe it or not—

THERE WAS MORE!

For though Tarsus was peopled with Hebrews and Egyptians and Greeks and Romans and just about anybody else you might want to mention, it was ruled by Rome.

And Rome was the greatest power in all the world!

So if you were born in Tarsus, a little Hebrew boy, you were more, far more than just a little Hebrew boy.

YOU WERE A ROMAN CITIZEN—A CITIZEN OF THE GREATEST POWER IN THE WORLD.

And you better believe it.

As a matter of fact, Saul's father never gave him a chance to forget it. So, if Saul said to his father, "But so-and-so is a faster runner than I am; he runs like the wind; his whole body is nothing but bone and muscle."

"Bah," his father would snort, "bone and muscle, indeed. He's scrawny, is what he is. He's nothing but skin and bones. He hasn't a muscle in his whole body. Forget him."

Or, if Saul would say, "But, Father, so-and-so is already taller than I am and we're exactly the same age and he's more filled out. He's going to be a much bigger man."

"Humbug," his father would say. "Fat is what he is, just plain fat. Just call him 'Fatso' and if he seems taller and bigger than you, it's just his swelled head. Forget him."

Or if Saul would say to his father, "Father, so-and-so can shoot an arrow better than I and he's better with a sling too."

"Bosh, and double bosh," his father would mutter. "And what good is that going to do him in life unless he decides to become a soldier? He may shoot an arrow straighter than you, but he's not as smart. Don't forget that."

Now there was one argument that Saul should have been able to win, but do you think he ever did?

Not a chance.

"But, Father," he would argue, and he used this argument more often than all the rest, "the other boys at school read faster than I do and they read faster because they can see better;

they can see the letters. My eyes are weak and I cannot see the letters as clearly."

"That is no excuse!" his father would bellow, for this was the argument that made him angrier than any of the others. "So your eyes are not quite as sharp as theirs; then hold your copybook closer to your eyes. Close— close—like this—see?" And he would thrust the copybook up so close to Saul's face that he nearly rubbed Saul's nose in it.

"Yes, Father, I see," Saul said obediently, though he didn't see at all. After all, if you had to hold your copybook so close to your face that your nose was practically touching it, then you must have weak eyes, no matter what his father said.

But after the oil lamp was blown out for the night and Saul's father was down the street, gossiping with the other men of the city, Saul and his mother would often sit quietly in the dark on the front steps of their house.

"But you can't be strong in everything," Saul's mother would say softly.

"But I am *smart*, Mother," he would argue.

"I can outsmart anybody in my class. I can argue better than anybody, and even though I can't win all the games, I know the rules better than anyone else. And I love God the best, and someday, Mother, I'm going to be the most important man for God in the world, and don't you forget it."

"I have no doubt that you will, Saul," his mother said. "But God is going to have to teach you many lessons first."

"Teach me!" Saul almost shouted. "Teach me what? What can He possibly teach me that I have not already learned?"

"Ah, my son," his mother sighed, "there are more lessons to be learned from God than what we learn in books. There is more to living than what is put into our heads."

"Such as what?" he argued. "What more could there possibly be in my head than is there already?"

"Ah, more," his mother went on, "much more. You see, we have minds, my son, and God has given you an excellent mind. But we need more than minds and bodies. There's the gift of kindness. There's the gift of sympathy

for others. There is the gift of patience,
learning to *wait* without being ill-tempered
when everything seems to be going wrong.
And there's the gift of humility."

"What? Humility?" he scoffed.

"Yes—the gift of being humble, of not
being stuck-up, of learning to know that you
are not better than everybody else. You might
be better at *some* things but no one can be
better at *everything*. You must learn that God
loves other people every bit as much as He
loves you. These are the things I want you to
remember after you've gone away and left our
home."

Ah, now at last she was on his favorite
subject—going away from home. Going away
to school.

"Ah, now you're talking about the things I
love to talk about," he said aloud, and his eyes
brightened as he shifted his seat on the step
and turned toward his mother. "Father says
that as soon as I finish my grades here I shall
be sent to Jerusalem to complete my education.
And I'll be studying under Gamaliel, the
greatest teacher in all the world."

"But, Saul—"

"I know, I know," Saul hurried on. "I know all about patience and humility and developing my character and all that sort of thing. You keep telling me and telling me and *telling me*. But there are other things, maybe more important, Mother. Father says I must learn a trade. I've decided to learn how to make tents. That's what I'll be—a tentmaker. I won't make that my life's work, of course. I'm much too smart for that, but if money ever runs out, I'll always be able to make a living."

He jumped to his feet for he saw his father coming up the street. He stooped to kiss his mother tenderly on the forehead. "Goodnight, Mother," he said. "I love you. And I'll try to remember all the things you said. I already have them in my head, you know."

"Good night, Egghead," she laughed, using Saul's nickname. "But remember, I warn you, if that egghead of yours swells much more than it has already, you might wind up being something you hadn't planned on."

He turned in the doorway. "And what's that?" he asked.

"A scrambled egg," she said, laughing.

He laughed too as he went indoors, for although he argued with his mother and sometimes grew weary of her lessons and patience and humility and kindness, he really loved her very dearly. For he had to admit that all the things she talked about she didn't just *talk* about. She *lived* them. She was patient. She was loving. She was kind. All these things she told him were wrapped up in one word, and that word is "love."

As he got ready for bed, Saul heard his mother and father talking softly as they sat in the doorway in the dark. And as he drifted off to sleep his mind was fairly popping with all sorts of ideas of the great life he was going to have and the great man he was going to be. He would learn how to make tents, of course, in case he ever had to support himself. Everybody should learn a trade—even an egghead.

But more important than that, he would go to Jerusalem and study under the greatest teacher in the world—Gamaliel. And from there on it would be only a short step to becoming perhaps one of the greatest, most powerful men in all Jerusalem. Why he might even be one of the members of the greatest court in the Hebrew religion—

THE GREAT SANHEDRIN.

If the time ever came when he had to learn those other things his mother talked about, he could pick them up quickly enough when the time came. Right now the most important thing was to be—

POWERFUL.

AND FAMOUS.

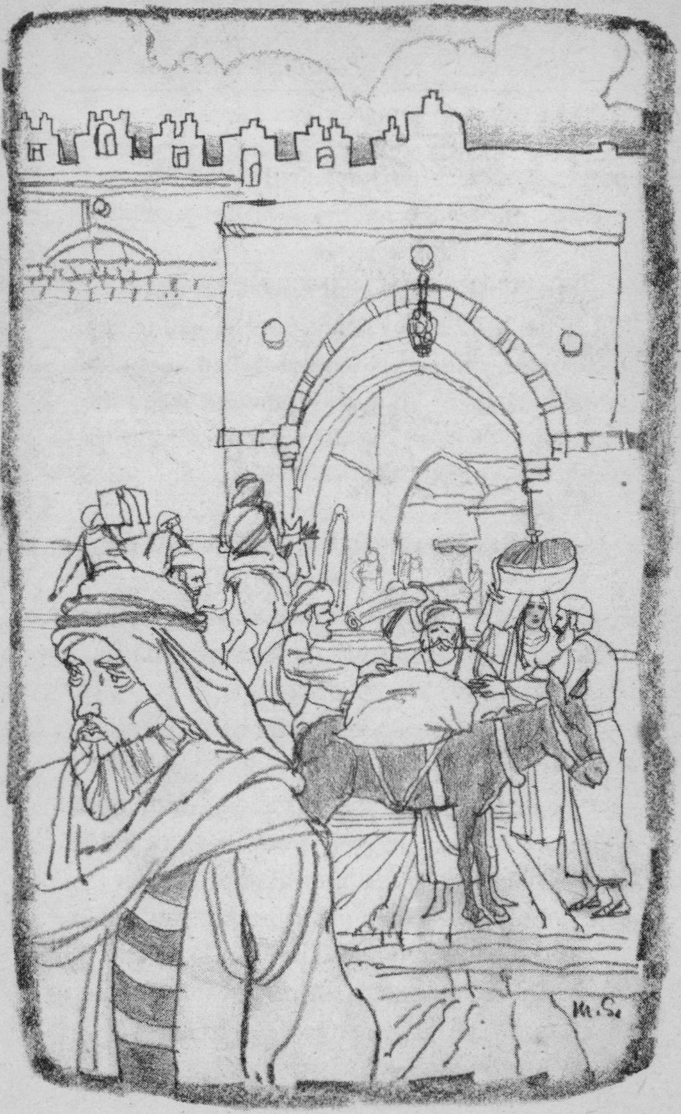

2

JERUSALEM!
"BUT WHAT'S GOING
ON?"

Jerusalem!

One of the most exciting cities in all the world!

Saul knew it well by now, for many years had passed since he had lain dreaming on his sleeping mat back home in Tarsus.

Now he was studying under the greatest teacher in all the world—Gamaliel. Saul got long letters from his father prodding him again and again to study, study, study. He got letters from his mother too, urging him to tell her everything, for she delighted in the tales he had to tell of all the places he had been and all the things he had done. She urged him to keep studying too. And he wrote back to her laughingly, saying that if he studied as much as each of them wanted him to, he might indeed become that scrambled egg they had laughed about that night.

Every time he was home for the holidays they sat for hours around the table after their meals, and on the steps of the doorway in the evenings, sometimes by the light of a buttery moon, sometimes with no moon at all where they could see only each other's shadows in the darkness.

As the years went by he grew taller, of course, but never quite as tall as he hoped he would. Nor did he ever fill out as did his boyhood friend his father had jokingly called "Fatso." And as the years went by he grew farther and farther apart from his parents. He never forgot the lessons they had taught, though, and he had not yet lost the idea that he was going to be one of the greatest and most famous men in the world, certainly one who loved God better than anyone. Indeed, it did look as though a lot of his boasting was true, for no one ever caught him in a sin. He knew every law in God's book—and kept them all.

He knew every law of the Sabbath, too.

The Sabbath was a quiet day and when Hebrews said "quiet," believe me they meant it. None of the women could cook on the Sabbath. Or bake. Baking always had to be done the day before because on the Sabbath you could not light a fire—not on your life.

Some of the Pharisees even debated whether the women could wash dishes on the Sabbath. For throwing the dishwater out would mean work and they were not allowed to work. After they quibbled about that for a while, they spent more months quibbling about the fact that the dishwater the women threw out might cause some weeds or plants to grow and that would be planting! Horrors! Surely no planting on the *Sabbath*! Any Pharisee worth his salt could quibble over that one for months—and Saul was a Pharisee to a fare-thee-well.

Some other things the Pharisees quibbled over were equally as silly. You couldn't, for instance, sew two stitches on the Sabbath. Now the idea that anybody could get anything mended with one stitch never entered their heads. Somehow it was all right to take one stitch, but it wasn't all right to take two.

Why, you couldn't even tie a knot unless it was the kind of knot that could be untied with one hand (try that one).

You couldn't catch a deer.

Or sow seed. Or plow.

You couldn't even *spit*. Why? Because if you did you might make a dent in the ground and it would be like plowing!

Now the really odd part about all this was that these were not laws God had made up at all. God had nothing to do with them. It was the *Pharisees* who had made them up. And in all Saul's studying and all his traveling and all his knowledge it had never once entered his head that these laws were *silly*. He was smart enough in things that counted with men, but he wasn't quite smart enough in many of the things that counted with God.

But in all his travels with his father during his boyhood, and later alone as a young man, he had never forgotten or changed his mind about one fact: Jerusalem was without a doubt the most exciting city in the world. The streets were crooked and winding. And they were lined with all kinds of shops that had open fronts. Almost everything for sale was spread right out in the streets.

Rugs. Silks and cottons of every color and description. Dates and fruits and grape leaves and spices and milk, and everything else you could imagine.

And besides looking at the goods, you had to watch where you were going. Peddlers threaded their way through the crowds with enormous trays of breads stacked several feet high on their heads—and never dropped a loaf.

And donkeys! You couldn't go four feet without bumping into a donkey. Or having one bump into you. They were loaded too—with dishes and pots and pans and jars of lotions and medicines and perfume.

The Temple was the most exciting place of all, of course. It was not HUMUNGOUS* as some buildings are today, but it was big enough to still be very impressive. It was not as beautiful as the first one King Solomon** built many long years ago. For down through

* That's really BIG!
** You can read about this Temple in 1 Kings 6.

the years and through many, many wars, the
Temple was destroyed time and time again
until it was a wonder that there was any
Temple there at all.

This Temple had been rebuilt by King
Herod who ruled Jerusalem in those days. He
had trained a thousand priests as masons
(stoneworkers) to build it. They had filled it in
with rubble where it was dented in and
propped it up with great stones where it sagged
and enclosed it with a huge wall of massive
stone blocks, some four feet high and fifteen
feet long.

It had an outer court and an inner court and
rooms inside where only the priests were
allowed to go. The great outer court was called
the court of the Gentiles,* and along the
insides of the walls were great porches with
huge columns supporting the roofs over them.
It was there that scholars gathered to learn, and
people collected to debate and argue.

But in spite of the fact that the Temple was
not as beautiful as when Solomon had first
built it, the huge cream-colored stones of

* People who were not *Hebrews*.

Herod's Temple dazzled on a sunny day. And they gleamed at night in the pale moonlight like a great jewel.

When Saul entered Jerusalem this particular morning, he did not notice any of these things. He went past all the shops and the donkeys and the loaves of bread without seeing them.

He went around the crooked streets. And any donkey who dared get in his way was shoved aside. The look of the scholar was gone from Saul's eyes and in its place was a look of a—*wild man*. For Saul—the great scholar—the great know-it-all—the man who had never done anything wrong in his life— had suddenly gone quite crazy.

There was only one thought in his mind as he trudged along through the crowds toward the Temple.

MURDER.

Now you could always count on Saul to do the unexpected. It had been anybody's guess what he would do next. But *this*?

It must have been something shocking to make him act this way.

Something very shocking indeed.

3

THIS MAN
CALLED JESUS

What happened was more than shocking. It was *mind*-boggling. And it had all begun with one man.

A man named Jesus.

Now what Jesus had done to turn the world upside down, He had not done overnight. In fact, it had been going on for years. He had gone around the countryside preaching about God's love. And the precious rule book the Pharisees had been working on for hundreds of years? Why, this man Jesus had just tossed it out as if it were nothing important at all.

All those rules about not spitting on the Sabbath or not tying a knot unless it could be untied with one hand or catching a deer or sowing a seed or plowing—

All those important rules the Pharisees had been spending their whole lives making up no longer important? Why how else could a man get right with God unless he kept all those rules?

And this Jesus had preached that nobody could get right with God, no matter how many rules he kept—nobody in all the world. And there was no way anybody under the sun could be perfect, no matter how many rules he kept.

And that wasn't all.

There was only one way anybody could get right with God. God had sent His Son—HIS VERY REAL ONLY SON—to live on the earth to preach and to teach. Then to be put to death to pay for the sins of every man and woman and boy and girl who had ever been born or ever would be born!

And that's not all.

Jesus had also said that *He was that Son*. He would die for the sins of the world and God His Father would raise Him up from the dead again. That would be God's great gift to all the people who believed!

And that's not all!

This Jesus had gone all about the land preaching and teaching this—and *healing* people. Yes! He had made blind people see again. And crippled people walk again.

And He had even brought some people back to life—after they had died!

Now that was indeed enough to shock you right out of your sandals and send you spinning backwards on the ground. In fact, many of the strictest Pharisees had done exactly that. They had tried to have Him captured, but He'd slithered through crowds of people like greased lightning. Nobody could catch Him.

So for three years while Jesus taught and preached it had been a game of "Catch me if you can." No matter how hard they tried to trick Him or catch Him or accuse Him, He would always slip out of their grasp and turn up someplace else, teaching.*

But catch Him they had, and they nailed Him on a cross and left Him there until He was dead.

* How they finally caught Him is a long and fascinating story. You can read about it in Luke 22.

And then they had put Him in a tomb and rolled a stone over it and put the governor's seal on it so that no one could open it.

And they set Roman guards outside to watch and guard the entrance to make *sure* no one could steal His body away.

Now that should have been the end of it.

But it wasn't.

For three days later the most amazing thing happened. The Roman guards guarding the tomb had been struck down like dead men, the huge stone had been rolled aside and the governor's seal had been broken.

And Jesus was gone!

"What!" Saul bellowed when the Pharisees told him this part of the story. "Gone—what do you mean 'gone'? Gone where?"

"That's the problem," people told him. "Nobody knew where. He was just *gone*."

"Bah," Saul bellowed, and "humbug," and he sounded just like his father. "*Somebody* stole His body away. We've got to get to the end of this problem, stop this nonsense at once."

"We'd like to stop it," the Pharisees told

him, "but there is just one little problem."

"What *problem*?!" Saul bellowed.

"The problem, Sir, is that He is still around."

"What do you mean He's still around?" Saul thundered, and he nearly tore his toga off to express his anger.

"People have seen Him," they told Saul. "He keeps appearing in different places. He even walks through locked doors and appears in rooms where His disciples* are. At least that's what they say."

"Oh, His disciples," Saul said, and he spat on the ground. "Silly men who followed Him everywhere and believed every word He said. Now that He's dead why don't the foolish disciples shut their mouths?"

"But that's the problem," they went on. "Now *they're* going about preaching and telling the people that everything He said about Himself was right, that He was indeed the Lord, that He was God Himself come to earth!"

---

* These were the men who had followed Jesus all through His ministry.

"Then lock them up!" Saul shouted. "Shut their mouths. Put them in jail."

"It's too late, Saul," they said, "because more and more people are beginning to believe them. The authorities lock them up and they escape from jail. People even say that God has sent guardian angels to help them escape and to protect them."

"But the Sanhedrin!" Saul shouted. "Can't they do something?"

"But even the Sanhedrin can't stop them," the men went on.

"What do you mean, the Sanhedrin can't stop them?" Saul said. "Isn't there anybody in the Sanhedrin important enough and powerful enough to stop them?"

"The most important and powerful members in the whole Sanhedrin said to leave these disciples alone. Because if they were wrong, the whole thing would soon blow over and everybody would soon forget it. But if they were right and this man Jesus was indeed the Son of God then nobody would be able to stop them anyway."

"And who is the important man who said

this?" Saul demanded.

"Gamaliel."

"*Gamaliel*!?!"

Saul was so angry by now that he would have spat on the ground except that he didn't have a drop of spittle left in his mouth. They waited in silence for him to get enough juice in his mouth to get his tongue a-wagging, but he could not seem to find a word to say. He just sat there on a bench outside one of the shops and stared furiously at the ground.

He's going to come up with something, they all thought as they waited. If anybody can do it, Saul can.

But Saul opened his mouth like a surprised guppy and closed it again. Not a sound came out.

And it wouldn't have mattered anyhow, for at that moment shouting arose from the outer courts of the Temple, almost like an explosion. People who had been just walking past in the streets now began to run, pushing donkeys aside and nearly upsetting the peddlers' tall trays of bread.

Saul and his friends jumped to their feet

and started to follow the crowd. They kept
their ears open, picking up what information
they could as they hurried along.

"The Sanhedrin is in session!"

"And it's no ordinary session
either—they're trying one of Jesus' followers."

"Who? Who?"

"Nobody seems to know."

"But it's a young man. One of their
leaders, and they've got him for sure this time.
They'll probably have him put to death!"

And there was murder written in their faces
as they shouted and jostled. Saul followed
along as best he could; he never said a word,
not one, but his thoughts were whirling.
"Whoever he is," he thought, *"it serves him
right. Whoever he is, I hope they get him."*

For although he did not shout, "Kill him!"
And he did not say a word—

There was murder in his heart.

4

"KILL THE SCOUNDREL!"
Acts 6:1—7:60

When Saul and his friends got to the court of the Sanhedrin the room was packed to the doors. The young man on trial was named Stephen.

And Stephen was in about as much trouble as any young man could be.

Stephen was one of the followers of Jesus. But he was more than that. He was a leader. There was something extra special about Stephen. He was so filled with the Spirit of God that he could not stop talking about his Lord.

But just talk about Him?

He talked about Him with such power that soon he was the gossip of the town. And he did more than just talk. The Bible tells us that he performed miracles and remarkable signs among the people.* This means that he did many of the things that Jesus Himself had done. He *healed* people. He made the blind see; he made the deaf hear; he made the crippled walk and he talked about Jesus and talked about Jesus and *talked* about Jesus. There was no end to it. Nobody could shut him up.

Everybody tried.

The Jews began to argue with him. But Stephen was so filled with the knowledge and the power of God that nobody was any match for him.

Finally, when they couldn't trip him up right out in the open, they tried ways that were a bit more sneaky. They hired men to spread gossip that Stephen had cursed Moses. And even *God*.

Of course, they were lies of the worst sort. They figured if they couldn't get him with the truth, they'd get him with lies.

So they dragged him on to the great

* Read Acts 6:8 in *The New Testament in Modern English*.

Sanhedrin, the highest Jewish court in the land, and put him on trial.

Saul stood in the back of the crowded room and listened to all this. He listened as one witness after another got up and told his lies, and each lie was worse than the last. They not only told the lies they had been *told* to tell, but they even added to their stories.

Saul stood in the back of the room believing every word he heard. *Why, the young scoundrel! How dare Stephen say such things?*

Finally the witnesses finished. The court session ended. Saul stared at the young man Stephen. Would he become flustered? Would he hang his head, beg for mercy?

Stephen did neither of these things. Instead, as Saul stared, a very remarkable thing happened.

Stephen's *face* seemed to change. Saul could scarcely believe his eyes. Stephen's face seemed to glow—like the face of an angel!* There was a great silence in the courtroom. Everyone waited.

Then finally the high priest broke the spell.

* Read Acts 6:15 in *The Living Bible*.

"Are these accusations true?" he said, turning to Stephen. Saul stared hard at Stephen. *Surely he'll sink to his knees now—the scoundrel.*

But that is not what happened.

Stephen started to speak and as he spoke, it was as if a spell of silence came over the entire courtroom. Stephen did nothing to defend himself. Instead he went back to the very beginning of the Hebrews' history. He told the people of God's great plan for them, how He had sent them prophet after prophet and leader after leader to show them the way He wanted them to go—and when they would not listen, God finally sent them His very own Son, Jesus Christ, a very part of God Himself.

And what did they do?

They crucified Him.

Saul sagged a little against the wall at this. Then he looked around the room. Every person in the room was grinding his teeth in rage. Every face in that room was twisted out of shape with anger.

But then Saul looked back at Stephen. Something strange was happening. Stephen was not looking *at* the people at all. He was looking *through* the people—he was looking *beyond* the people. Saul expected a brilliant argument; surely Stephen would say something in his favor. After all, he was about to be killed.

Instead Stephen cried out, "I see the heavens opened! And I see Jesus *standing— standing at the very right hand of God*."

If Saul was angry before, he was angrier now than he had ever been in all his life.

How *dare* this young man Stephen say such a bold thing?

Saul turned to the people next to him to say this very thing, but he never got a chance—for the whole court was filled with such shouting as he had never heard before in his life. It was without a doubt the noisiest session the Sanhedrin had ever known.

Before Saul could even voice an opinion, everyone in the court tore into Stephen. They dragged him into the outer courts of the Temple. They dragged him into the streets toward the East Gate.

Saul followed them willingly, eager for this killing. He followed them all the way to the

East Gate of Jerusalem. Outside the East Gate
the crowd dragged Stephen and threw him
down to the ground. No doubt about it, it was
going to be a stoning. Saul stood there waiting
for it, expecting it, wanting it. This was a
stoning the rascal Stephen well deserved.

The official witnesses took off their outer
robes* so they'd be free to sling those deadly
stones with greater accuracy. They laid their
outer garments down in a pile.

Now the law in those days said that
someone had to guard those outer garments so
they would not be stolen and taken away.

This was when Saul came to life again.

He stepped away from the crowd and
toward the pile of robes. "I will guard the
garments," he said. And he stood there, his
arms folded, his face filled with anger and
murder. He stood there on guard as if he were
guarding God Himself as he prepared to watch
this young rascal be killed.

Go to it, Saul thought. *It serves him right.*

Then one of the officials picked up the first

---

* It was a Jewish law, the official witnesses had the privilege (?)
of throwing the first stones.

stone, the biggest one he could find, and slung it with all his might. It hit Stephen in the chest and he sagged to his knees. Then another stone hurled through the air. It hit Stephen in the side of the head and he crumbled. It was a signal for the crowd to join in and they picked up rocks and they screamed in rage as they threw them at Stephen.

Stephen lay on the ground, his arms outstretched.

And he cried out.

He did not cry out in pain or protest.

He cried out only twice. The first time, he said, "Lord Jesus, receive my spirit!"

And then, "Lord, don't hold this sin against them. They don't know what they're doing."

And then he died.

It was all over.

Good, thought Paul. *The scoundrel is dead!*

5

JOURNEY UPSIDE DOWN
Acts 8:1—9:9

The stoning was over.

But Saul was not through. He had only just begun. "What are these disciples of Jesus doing?" he wanted to know. "How are they spreading this craziness?"

"They are meeting secretly," his friends told him. More and more people are believing that Jesus Christ is God. It is spreading like wildfire, and not only through Jerusalem, but through all the country. There is nothing we can do about it."

"But where are they meeting?" Saul demanded.

"They are meeting secretly in homes, and not just here in Jerusalem; they have gone far abroad. They have gone as far as Damascus."

"*Damascus!*" Saul shouted.

"Yes," they told him. "They call themselves *the church*—and there seems to be no stopping them."

"Well," Saul said finally, "there's one person who can stop them. *I'll* stop them. I'll root them out of their homes. I'll get documents and letters to give me the authority to go wherever I want and root them out. In fact, I think I'll start with Damascus if they've gone that far."

They took one look at him and realized that he meant every word he said.

A few days later Saul put his plan into action. He went to the Sanhedrin and asked them for letters of authority to go wherever he wanted to root these "church people" out of their homes, drag them to the East Gate and get them stoned.

And the first place he wanted to go was Damascus.

He got the authority all right, with no trouble at all. He was a highly respected student of the great Gamaliel.

In a few weeks he was ready to go.

And *raring* to go.

The officials were picked to go with him
on this journey. It was going to be the greatest
journey, he figured, that he would ever take in
his life. And it was.

But not quite the way he expected.

It was before dawn when the little band of
officials led by Saul began their journey. The
donkeys were loaded, their saddlebags filled
with canteens of water and provisions. Saul
gave the order to start and the little caravan
was on its way. The men's faces were grim.*

Off they went, clumping silently along the
desert sand, hardly speaking. The only sound
at all was the clop, clop of the hoofs of the
donkeys. They stopped only when they had to
stop to rest, so anxious were they to get on
their way and get this exciting mission
accomplished. Saul's eyes were squinted
against the sun in hatred.

Now, he thought he was at last going to
become what he had studied all his life to
become—a person of great fame and power

* From Gloomsville.

who would get credit for stopping all this
nonsense about this person Jesus. He, Saul,
would go down in history as the man who
upheld the laws of God. Nobody—but nobody
in all the world would be as important as he!

Damascus, he kept thinking. *It is in
Damascus where I will at long last be famous
and powerful as I've always dreamed I'd
be—as my father told me I would be.*

When Damascus finally appeared in the
distance, its great gray walls shimmering in the
heat, Saul urged his donkey on. He would ride
into the city in style, he thought, and everyone
who saw his face would be *pulverized* with
fear. For, of course, everyone would realize at
once what a powerful and important person he
was.

It was then that it happened.

Suddenly—a great light!

A light more powerful and more brilliant
than any light he had ever seen in all his
life—a light even more powerful than the sun
itself!

It blazed upon him like a great spotlight.
He started to call out to his donkey to stop,

but the donkey did not need to be told. He was paralyzed with fear too. He stopped in his tracks.

In fact, he stopped so suddenly that Saul fell right over his neck, slid down the front of his nose and landed on the ground like a sack of potatoes. The other men around him stopped their animals too and stood there in amazement and fear, for they had heard—what was it?

Thunder?

A voice?

They did not know.

They knew only that they were standing in the presence of some great and terrible power they had never never known before.

It was a voice all right, but Saul was the only one who heard it and understood it. It was a voice—calling him by his name!

"Saul," it said, and again, "Saul—"

Saul finally managed to get his face out of the sand and get on his elbows and turn his face upward. He knew he didn't look like a very powerful and important person at that moment; he knew only one thing: that voice was talking to him—and he had better *listen*.

He waited, trembling, for the voice to go on.

It did.

"Saul," the voice went on, "why are you fighting against me like this?"

Saul spit some sand out of his mouth and swallowed hard. When he tried to speak, his voice did not come out powerful or important at all. It was more like a frightened squeak.

"Who are you?" he said at last.

"I am the very One you have been fighting against. *I AM JESUS*. Why are you fighting me?"

"JESUS!?!"

Saul started to get up to his knees, but they were so weak, he slid back down again and just lay there in the sand. And in one blinding moment all his old beliefs, all his dreams, everything he had ever been taught, and every plan he had ever made went down the drain as if you had pulled the plug out of a bathtub. He just lay there trembling in the dust. Every argument he had ever learned in all his life was of no use to him now, for the voice that was speaking to him was indeed the voice of

Jesus. And Jesus was indeed the Son of God. In fact, the very God Himself.

"Now get up," the voice said.

Saul staggered to his feet.

"But, Lord," he began.

"Don't but me," the Lord said. "And don't try to second-guess me. Just do what you're told. I've had a hard enough time with you already."

"Yes, Lord," Saul said meekly.

"All right, now," the Lord said back, "from here on, stop making your own plans. I'll make your plans for you. And my first plan for you is to go into Damascus and it is there that you will be told what I want you to do next."

"Yes, Lord. Yes, Lord. Yes—" Saul kept repeating, trying to rub the sand from his eyes.

Meanwhile, his companions were babbling like idiots. They were still so frightened they could scarcely stand.

"Explain to us what happened," they insisted.

"I don't know any answers," Saul said back. "I only know one thing—the voice that

just spoke to me was the voice of Jesus
Christ—the voice of God Himself. Everything
Jesus said about Himself was true.

"You'll have to lead me," Saul continued.
"I have sand in my eyes. I can't see."

They took their kerchiefs and began to dab
at his eyes. Then they stopped and stared at
each other in horror. Then finally one of them
said it.

"There is no sand in your eyes, Saul."
And then he realized the horrible truth.
HE WAS BLIND!

6

FRIEND OR ENEMY?
Acts 9:10-18

Something strange was going on outside
Damascus, all right. This group of
"frightening" people led by Saul was expected
to storm the gates and show their papers of
authority and demand entrance. But now they
were about as frightening as a bunch of
sandbags.

Astonishing!

"What shall we do, Sir?" Saul's officials
asked him.

"We'll do exactly what God told me to
do," Saul answered. "He told me to go into
Damascus and there He would tell me what
more He wants me to do."

They stared at Saul the way you'd stare at

a donkey that had just decided to talk.

"I am blind," he went on.

They looked at each other and sighed. Surely Saul had lost his wits. But he was, after all, still the boss, so they took him by his hands and led him carefully along the sandy road toward the great gates of Damascus.

Now if you think something strange was going on *outside* Damascus, wait until you hear what was going on inside.

Inside Damascus was a disciple of Jesus whose name was Ananias. Ananias had heard about the terrible Saul of Tarsus and all the mischief he had done in Jerusalem. The gossip had come pouring into Damascus with the caravans and with the refugees about the suffering that was going on. The tales were scary enough to make any believer shiver in his sandals, and Ananias did not wish to run headlong into trouble. No siree, he intended to love the Lord, tell people about Him all right, but he also intended to stay as far away from any persecutors as he could get.

This is what Ananias had in mind.

But this was NOT what God had in mind.

Indeed, God was about to give Ananias the surprise of his life.

Soooooo—

Ananias lay asleeping, feeling as safe and snug as a mouse in a house where no cat lives—when suddenly—

He heard God's voice too.

"Ananias—Ananias—*Ananias*—"

"Yes, Lord," Ananias said, struggling up on one elbow, for he knew that it was the voice of God speaking to him.

"Ananias," the voice said, "wake up. There is something I want you to do."

"Yes, Lord, what is it? Anything— anything!"

Ananias was fully awake now, sitting up on his sleeping mat.

"Ananias, I want you to get up and go over to Straight Street—"

"Yes, Lord. Straight Street, Lord. Got it, Lord."

"Go to Straight Street and find the house of a man named Judas—"

"Yes, Lord. Judas. Got it."

"Knock on the door. Ask for a man who is staying there."

"Yes, Lord. And who is the man I should ask for?"

"The man," the voice of the Lord came back, "is Saul of Tarsus."

SAUL OF TARSUS!?!?!?!?!

"Did you say Saul of Tarsus, Lord? Did I hear you right?"

"Yes, I said Saul of Tarsus, for he is praying to me right now. He is there resting. He is blind. And don't worry about it, Ananias. I have already prepared the way, for I have already given *him* a vision of *you* and I have told him that you will place your hands on him and pray for him and restore his sight."

For the first time a little shiver of fear started up the spine of poor Ananias and went clear up to his head. He tried to get his thoughts together, but the little prickles of fear kept getting in the way.

"You did say Saul of Tarsus, didn't you, Lord?" he said, and his voice came out in a squeak.

"Yes, I did," the voice came back, "and

that's exactly who I meant—Saul of Tarsus.
He is on Straight Street—"

"Yes, I got it, Lord, I got it," said
Ananias, fully awake at last. "Straight Street.
The house of the man named Judas."*

"All right, Lord," Ananias said. "All
right." He got up from his sleeping mat and
began to shiver out of his nightclothes. "But,"
he sputtered, as if God did not know it
already, "I've heard of the terrible things that
man has done to Christians in Jerusalem, and
he has come here for nothing but mischief,
Lord. He even has authority from the chief
priests to arrest every believer in Damascus
and drag them back to Jerusalem." Ananias
shimmied into his outer garments and put on
his sandals.

"I don't mean to question you, Lord,"
Ananias said, "but these things are true. I
know; I've been around here for a long time."

"And I've been around here a lot longer,"
God said. "So don't question what I say. I

* Now we do not know exactly who this "Judas" was. The Bible
does not tell us. But we do know that he must have been another
secret believer and that God knew exactly what He was doing
when He had Saul's friends take him there so Judas could give
him shelter.

have chosen this man, Saul, to take the gospel to all the nations and before kings—as well as to the Jews—so just stop quibbling. Do as I say."

"I'm sorry, Lord. I'm sorry," Ananias muttered half to himself and lighted his little oil lamp and stumbled toward the door.

But when he opened it he stopped in his tracks. He did not need his oil lamp, it was already daylight.

He walked swiftly through the streets, his head down—until he got to the street called Straight.

It was then that another little trickle of fear started up his spine again. "Saul of Tarsus!" Had he really heard God correctly?

But then, as suddenly as he said it, the fear was gone. And a great feeling of peace settled over his heart, and a feeling of the power of God came into him again. He skipped along the street, looking for a house that belonged to a man called Judas. When he got there he knocked at the door loudly and stood there trembling—but now with excitement— impatiently waiting for someone to open it.

When someone did, he bowed politely.

"Is this the home of Judas?" he asked. "I have been sent to this house by God Himself. I must see Saul of Tarsus—at once."

He expected an argument, but he got none. They let him in without a word and led him to a room in the back of the house. They pulled the curtain aside and let him in.

Ananias wasted no time. Saul of Tarsus was propped up on his sleeping mat. His eyes were open, but it was plain that he could not see. And then Ananias began to talk and the words that came out of him did not seem to be his words at all. They were the very words of God Himself.

"Brother Saul," he said. "Brother Saul." And he went over and knelt by Saul's sleeping mat.

Brother Saul! Imagine. Ananias's worst enemy—*Brother Saul!*

But Ananias did not think of that at all. "Brother Saul," he said again softly, and he put his hands on Saul's head. "The Lord Jesus—the very Lord who spoke to you on your journey here—has sent me to see you," and before Saul could answer he went on, "so that you would be filled with the very Spirit of God Himself—and so that you may get your sight back."

And then—

It was as if scales had fallen from Saul's sightless eyes. He looked at Ananias eyeball to eyeball.

He could see!

And the two of them just clasped hands and looked at each other in love! They were no longer enemies. To them there was only one important thing that mattered now.

What a turnabout!

And what was going to happen now?

And what excitement and adventure lay ahead?

7

"THIS MAN IS DANGEROUS!"
Acts 9:18-26; Galatians 1:17,18

What a turnabout!

It was enough to make you dizzy.

Saul was not the same man. The people who had known him before could scarcely believe it. In the first place, he insisted on being baptized, and he *was* baptized—in the name of *Jesus* who was now his Lord.

"Are you going to preach?" his officials asked him. "Are you going around to the synagogues in Damascus and tell everybody about this new thing?"

"No," Saul said quietly. "I am not ready to preach yet, for I have been so wrong about my God. All my life I've been taught that the only way to get right with God was to be *perfect*.

Now I realize that I never have been perfect
and I never will be. Not without the Lord
Jesus to help me. I'm going off somewhere to
talk to Jesus and ask Him questions. I'm going
to find out where and how I've been so wrong
all my life."

And that's exactly what he did. He took a
donkey loaded with provisions and he went off
all by himself into the deserts of Arabia to be
alone with his new Lord who had met him so
unexpectedly on the road into Damascus.* The
Bible does not tell us exactly how long he
stayed there, but it was a long, long time,
perhaps as long as three years. And when he
came back—

He began to preach. Did he ever begin to
preach! He preached in houses. He preached
on street corners. He preached in the
synagogues. He told *everyone* about Jesus. The
people crowded about to hear what this new
Saul had to say—and the Jews who had
believed he was wrong before—now began to
realize he was right! Aha!

* Paul tells us about Arabia much later in his letter to the
Galatians (1:17,18).

BUT—!

The Jews who had believed he was right
*before** now believed he was *wrong*. They
argued with him. They shot questions at him to
make him prove that these new things he was
saying were the truth. And with every question
he could come back with proof that Jesus was
the Christ. And slowly, slowly—

More and more people began to believe.

And more and *more*—

New believers cropped up everywhere. And
Saul became powerful—

Until—WHAM! It happened.

The Jewish leaders decided to take action.
This nonsense had gone quite far enough.

"This man is dangerous," they whispered to
each other. "We must do away with him."

And so they began to make plans to
capture Saul and finish him off.

They talked about it so much that Saul's
friends finally got wind of it.

They scurried about secretly listening to see
if they could find out what sort of plot Saul's

---

* Getting "right with God" to these Jews meant keeping a lot of
silly laws written by men.

enemies were planning against him.

The news was not good. In fact, the news was *terrible*. For Saul's enemies had posted guards outside the city gates. There wasn't a chance in the world that they could possibly sneak him out. Or *was* there?

As you know (or perhaps I forgot to tell you), Damascus was a walled city with gates that were heavily guarded. And these walls were so thick that houses were built atop them. And in *some* of these houses lived people who believed in Jesus. Now one dark night when the moon was just a sliver—

Inside one of those houses Saul's friends were waiting and watching. Near one of the windows was a huge basket with ropes tied through it and around it. They popped Saul into the basket and he sat there clinging to the sides. And they—hup!—hoisted the basket up on the windowsill.

A group of Saul's followers waited on the ground outside the city wall, looking up at that dark window. And then—

The signal was given. Saul's friends in the house slid the basket quietly over to the very edge of the windowsill and two men on either side got a tight hold on the ropes.

"Shhhh," they said, as they carefully lowered it off of the windowsill until the only thing that was supporting the basket now was their strong hands on the ropes.

"Easy, easy, let him down easy."

The basket began to slide down the wall.

"Ooops," they whispered. And "ugh" they groaned quietly as their knuckles scraped the stone wall outside the window.

Down, down, down the basket went until at last it was nearly at the bottom. Saul's friends were standing there, their arms outstretched, groping for the basket so it would not hit the ground with a thud. They grabbed it and gently lowered it to the ground.

Saul was free at last. He uncrouched himself and straightened up painfully. His friends helped him to his feet, for his knees were so stiff he could hardly get them unbent. No one said a word. They hoisted Saul up on one of the donkeys and quietly, very quietly, the little group sneaked off into the night.

And silently, very silently, they crept away

into the darkness. Back down the same sandy
road Saul had traveled years before on his way
into Damascus with murder in his heart. He
passed the spot where he had fallen from his
donkey and God had blinded him with His
light and with His glory. Saul could only guess
at the spot in the darkness, but he imagined
where it had been and he thought in his heart,
*This is the spot—the very spot—where Jesus
appeared to me and changed my life*. He
looked down at the sandy road, his eyes
blinded now with tears rather than blindness.

No one traveling with him said a word.

No one believed they were safe yet. It was
miles before they dared to whisper softly to
each other and then to talk.

God had protected them! They were safe.

They were off to Jerusalem.

But they were also off to—what?

Danger?

Sudden death?

Imprisonment?

What was ahead of them?

Well, I cannot tell you now, but I shall tell
you later if you just read on.

The most exciting part of Saul's life was
still ahead!

8

NEW FRIENDS FROM OLD ENEMIES
Acts 9:27-30

Jerusalem again!

During most of the journey Saul was silent, thinking. How would people greet him? Would they believe that he really had changed? Would the old disciples who had followed Jesus so closely believe him? Would they accept him as an apostle too?*

By the time he got to one of the big main gates of Jerusalem, his mind was in a tailspin, for he saw the great city as he had never seen it before. The crowded, crooked streets were there—and all the same old sights and smells. But somehow it was not the same at all. These were the streets where Jesus had walked.

And off there in the distance, on the Mount of Olives, was the very place where Jesus had

* The disciples were now called *Apostles*, remember?

slept at night with His disciples, and talked with them and told them all about God and all about Himself. And then beyond in the distance, the mountains—how many times had Jesus Himself looked up at those mountains and talked with God His Father? Saul's heart just nearly burst with love as he thought about all these things.

What would the apostles' reaction be?

If you're thinking that their reaction would be "Ugh!" you are quite right.

For Saul, now a believer in Jesus, went to a gathering of *other* believers in Jesus—and got the cold shoulder!

The very people who should have welcomed him with open arms were suspicious of him.

They were afraid of him.

They simply did not believe him.

But wait!

One of them did. "I am Barnabas," he said, coming toward Saul with his arms outstretched. He was a big man, but gentle —sort of like the favorite uncle who

comes to visit and brings you little presents
and loves to tell you stories. "And this is my
nephew, John Mark," he went on, drawing a
young man up close. "He is young. He is
eager to serve the Lord Jesus. He will be one
of your friends. And here's Peter," he said, as
he called to another man to come forth.

Peter was a big man with a craggy* face,
burnt black by the sun.

"Peter is a fisherman," Barnabas said, "or
rather, he *was* a fisherman. He was one of the
very first disciples of the Lord Jesus and he's
eager to help you."

Peter came forward and grasped Saul's
shoulders until they hurt.

"Oh, yes," Barnabas went on, "and here is
James, the very brother of our Lord."

Suddenly they were all talking at once.

In the end it turned out that Peter and his
wife invited Saul to stay in their home and rest
up a bit until they all decided just what the
Lord wanted them to do.

And Saul began to preach, and as he
preached, it was plain to see that the old

* All crinkled up in little creases.

enemy, the old thunderbolt, the old terror, was indeed a changed man.

He preached so boldly and argued with the Jews so brilliantly that—you guessed it.

Some of the Jewish leaders plotted to kill him.

What? Again? Yes. Again!

But again he had his little band of friends to help him, and this time they sneaked him away to—of all places—

TARSUS! His old hometown.

"You will not be forgotten," they called out to him as they left him safely outside Tarsus. "We will send for you as soon as the Lord gives us directions."

"Don't worry, Saul," Barnabas called out in good-bye. "You will be hearing from us!"

Saul called back his "thank you's" but he left them with a great sadness in his heart, for he had learned to love them very much. He had a feeling in his heart, though, that the most exciting part of his life was still ahead of him.

But meanwhile—what would Tarsus be like?

9

JOURNEY INTO THE PAST
Acts 11:22-25

Tarsus!

Saul's old hometown—the great city he had left so many long years ago. The news had dribbled in ahead that he was coming, of course, and his old friends were there to greet him—and so were his parents!

But things were different.

His mother's old sparkle was gone.

She no longer joked with him on the steps of a summer evening. She no longer teased him about the fact that if his "egghead" got any bigger it would burst and he would become a "scrambled egg." They did not seem to have the same things to laugh about any more.

And his father? Grim!

It was a few days before Saul realized what was wrong.

It was not that his parents had changed. It was that he—Saul himself—had changed. He was no longer the eager boy who had left to study under Gamaliel, who went off to seek his fortune. And he was not the famous and brilliant man his father had expected him to be. He was a refugee, hopping from town to town, escaping barely by the skin of his teeth because people were forever plotting to kill him.

But that was not the worst of it.

He was no longer the cocksure person he once had been. He was no longer bawling about rules or quibbling about whether or not you could spit on the ground on the Sabbath.

He was the worst of all things, in his father's sight—a believer in Jesus!

He not only believed in Jesus, but he loved Him—and was traveling about preaching about Him and talking about Him and trying to get others to love Him too.

Ah, the arguments he had with his father.

The cold shoulders he got from his neighbors
and his former friends. The long silences he
got from his mother as he watched her sad
eyes. And the scorn he got from his very own
synagogue in which he used to be so welcome.
They laughed at him. They scolded him. They
spat upon him. They chased him out of the
synagogue. They ordered him whipped.

But the worst part was in his own home,
for although his parents at first accepted him as
their own son—they—even they—finally
rejected him.

But Saul kept on "keeping on." He turned
to his trade of tentmaking so he would not
have to ask any money from anyone—even his
own family. He did something else too.

He went down to the river with the rest of
the athletes and stripped off his clothes and
exercised.

He did everything possible to keep his
body in the best shape he could.

And it worked. His body was slim and
strong and his muscles were as hard as steel.

He thought about Jesus constantly.

He talked to Jesus.

And waited.

Whatever was to come, he was ready for it.

And finally—it came!

A message from Barnabas!

Remember Barnabas? Oh, joy!

Barnabas, Saul's dear friend from Jerusalem—the one who had stood up for him and introduced him to the other believers in Jesus.

Saul read the message, his heart pounding with excitement.

But it was not from Jerusalem.

It was from Antioch, the capital of Syria.

Yes, the church had spread all the way to Antioch. In fact, it was growing so fast that Barnabas needed help. Would Saul come and help him?

Would Saul come and help him?!?

Saul could hardly wait to leave.

He knew that he was leaving Tarsus, his own hometown, in disgrace.

But he still left joyfully. He was back on the track again!

10

ENCOUNTER WITH A SORCERER
Acts 11:26-30; 12:25; 13:1-12

"Antioch, here I come," Saul's heart sang as he rushed to meet Barnabas. What a great place to work and to tell people about Jesus!

Antioch was the third greatest city of the Roman world, and it had broad streets and palaces and temples and huge stadiums where athletic events and circuses took place—but it had back streets, too, crooked and narrow and poor. So, though it was called "Antioch, the Beautiful and the Golden," there was plenty of ugliness there too.

But what a place to tell people about Jesus!

Saul and Barnabas got to work, their hearts singing with joy. The whole place was humming with believers in Jesus. In fact, it

was in Antioch that they were first called
Christians. Actually, the people meant it as a
sort of a nickname because of the name of
Jesus Christ. "Those Christ folks," they'd call
them.

But things were surely looking up for Saul.
He had many friends now who loved him. He
had homes in which to stay where he was
welcome and he and Barnabas were accepted
as two important members of the church. In
fact, they were selected to go back to
Jerusalem to take grain to the people there, for
the crops around Jerusalem had been poor, and
the people there were hungry. Suddenly, Saul
had more friends than he knew what to do
with.

It was when they got to Jerusalem that it
happened.

They had brought Barnabas's young
nephew, John Mark, with them. They were
meeting with a group of church leaders and
while they were praying—

Suddenly the Holy Spirit of God spoke to
them, "I have a special job I want Saul and
Barnabas to do," He said. "I want them to

travel. I want them to become *missionaries*."

Missionaries! Why, it was the first time in all the world anyone had ever heard of such a thing.

So Saul and Barnabas took John Mark* along with them and left from Antioch's busy port at Seleucia.

There were a lot of good-byes. And prayers.

Saul and Barnabas and John Mark were on their way!

Off to the island of Cyprus they sailed. And there, from one town to another, they preached their way clear across the whole island until they reached Paphos. Can you imagine what happened when they got to Paphos? They were invited right into the governor's** palace to speak!

Imagine!

As Barnabas and Saul walked up the broad avenue that led to the palace they looked like anything but ambassadors for the King. They looked more like a couple of merchants

* John Mark was Barnabas's nephew.
** Actually he was a proconsul.

peddling their wares who should have never been let in the front doors. But march up they did, their heads held high, past the palace guards, up the great hallways and into the enormous room where the governor sat on a little platform, on a large marble throne.

They stood before the governor straight and tall, their eyes flashing. And he asked them to tell him who this God was—and who this Jesus was. There were many people standing about—high officials, soldiers, guards—and one man who sent a little prickle of warning up Saul's spine. Barnabas felt Saul stiffen and looked over in the same direction and saw him too. The man was glaring back at them with hate and rage in his eyes. His name was Elymas.

And he was very strong and influential in the kingdom.

There was only one thing wrong with that.

He was a sorcerer.

A fake prophet!

Saul and Barnabas looked back at the governor.

"I want to hear what you were teaching,"

the governor said pleasantly. And they both began to explain. They told him the marvelous story of Jesus and His love for them, for him, the governor, too. And with every word they said, the governor's interest grew. He leaned forward on his throne. The Bible tells us he was "listening with much pleasure."

But with every word they said, the fury of the sorcerer increased. His eyes seemed to spit sparks of rage. Once he took a step forward and then stopped himself. It was an unthinkable thing to interrupt someone who was having an audience with the governor. But finally he could contain himself no longer.

"They lie," he cried out.

Suddenly there was a great silence. Everyone had been shocked almost out of his sandals. The governor looked at the sorcerer with amazement.

"They are lying," the sorcerer said. He was shrieking now. "Do not listen to them. Do not believe them! Their message is foolishness! If you believe them . . ." He stopped suddenly, the spittle dribbling down his chin in his fury. Everyone was staring at him. Everyone knew what he meant. For if the governor indeed did believe them, the sorcerer's influence would be finished. He would no longer be a man of power.

Then Paul* spoke for the first time. He did not shout. He did not need to, for the sorcerer had stopped screaming and everybody in the room was just standing there in stunned silence, listening.

"You son of a devil," Paul said. "You villain, full of every kind of trickery—yes, an enemy to all that is good. Isn't it time you stop this nonsense? You may be able to fool everybody in this court, but you will never fool Jesus, and you well know it."

The sorcerer's knees began to knock together. All the rage had gone from his eyes and in its place was fear. He opened his mouth to speak, but no word came out.

Words came out of Paul though, and though he spoke quietly, they came out with such power that there was no doubt in anybody's mind that they were words straight from God Himself.

* From here on Saul was called Paul. See Acts 13:9.

"And now," Paul said, "God is about to punish you. So that there may be no doubt that it is from God's hand—and not mine, you will be stricken for a while with blindness."

Everyone looked at the sorcerer in wonder and fear and suddenly—

A mist began to go over the sorcerer's eyes. The room got darker and darker until within a few moments he could see nothing at all. He groped around for someone's hand. Two of the guards in the room jumped to his side immediately, took him by the hand, and helped him out of the room.

There was no doubt about Paul's leadership now, nor about his power.

But did he quit, call it a day, settle down on this comfortable island and decide that from then on he would take life easy?

Not on your life!

There is much still to come.

11

UPS AND DOWNS
Acts 13:13—16:12

Paul and his friends continued on over mountains, through valleys, from town to town—

Pamphylia—Perga—Antioch—(another Antioch).*

It was along about this time that young John Mark decided to quit and go back home to Jerusalem. We don't know why he did it—whether he was homesick, or lovesick, or just plain scared. But don't be too hard on young John Mark. For he is the one who later on wrote the Gospel of Mark.

Anyhow, when they finally got to this "other Antioch," which was in Pisidia, they went to the synagogue.

* What? You're having trouble with the names of these cities? Well, just think. All you have to do is read them. They had to *travel* through them.

Now it was a custom in those days to allow visitors to speak in the synagogue if they cared to, so the synagogue officials said to Paul, "If you have any word of instruction for us, come up and give it."

And that was all Paul needed.

"Men of Israel," he said, "I want to tell you a story—a history of your own people."

"Ah," they thought, "this is going to be interesting."

And then Paul began. He told them the story of the Israelites and they listened, oh, so proudly.

Then he told them about the promised Messiah. The promise that Jesus would come.

"Yes, yes, go on." They wanted to hear more.

Then he told them of Jesus and how He had died for them and how God had raised Him from the dead, and that all who believed in Him could be right with God—which was something their Jewish laws could never do—why they had never heard of such a thing!

And they invited Paul and Barnabas back to speak the very next Sabbath.

And what's more the next Sabbath the synagogue was packed out. Almost the entire city turned out to hear Paul preach the word of God.

But there was one little problem.

Many of them were Gentiles.

And this was when the trouble began. The angry Jewish leaders argued with Paul. They jumped on every word he said; they cursed; they tried to shout him down.

And—you guessed it. Paul and Barnabas were finally run out of town.

They kept on going to Iconium, and in Iconium the story was the same.

They went on to Lystra, Derbe—

And the farther they went, the farther they got from civilization.

Now at last Paul knew what it was like to be chased. He knew what it had been like for Stephen. He knew what it was like to be whipped and stoned and threatened, and to be made to run for his very life. And now, at last, he realized what his mother had meant those long years ago during those quiet talks in the doorway of their home.

There are many, many lessons you cannot learn from books. There are many, many lessons God has to teach you through living.

And Paul and Barnabas never knew from one day to the next what kind of lessons they were going to learn.

One was a lesson they would not soon forget, for it was a total surprise.

It was while they were back in Lystra. Paul was preaching. And everyone was listening. There was hardly a sound except the sound of Paul's voice as he told them all about Jesus, but there was one man listening whom Paul especially noticed—a cripple. It was plain to see that those feet had been crippled from the time the poor man was born. Paul went on preaching.

But then suddenly—

He stopped right in the middle of a sentence, looked down into the man's eyes and shouted, "Get up on your feet!"

Everyone stopped, stunned, and then they shouted in amazement as the crippled man got to his feet and walked!

"These men are gods!" the people shouted.

"They are Jupiter and Mercury—come back to earth!"

And they danced in the streets. And the local priests of the temple Jupiter brought out garlands of flowers. They sacrificed the oxen at the city gate.

But were Paul and Barnabas happy about all this? Indeed they were *not*.

They ran out among the people, jumping up and down, and ripping their clothing. "Men!" they shouted, "have you gone mad?"

But the people only tried to hoist them up on their shoulders and shout the louder.

Paul and Barnabas did not give up though. In the midst of all that celebration they kept on telling the people they were *not* gods. They were simply human beings like everybody else—and they had come only to tell people about Jesus.

"My mother told me," Paul chuckled as he unrolled his sleeping mat that night, "that I was an 'egghead' and warned me not to get too stuck-up, but she never told me that I'd be mistaken for a god."

Barnabas chuckled too as he rolled over on

his side on his sleeping mat.

Of course the "easy life" did not last. For some of the Jews* followed them and stirred up trouble—and Paul and Barnabas were stoned—again! But did they give the whole idea up as a bad mistake?

They did not! THEY WENT ON!

To Derbe.

Lystra.

Iconium.

Antioch.

Pisidia, Pamphylia, Perga, Attalia.

Tired?

Hang on!

Antioch.

Jerusalem.

Back again to Antioch.

Are you tired yet?!?

Well so were they, probably. But after they had rested up a bit they decided to go off on another missionary journey. Only this time they went off in different directions. Barnabas wanted to take young John Mark along again, but Paul did not, for young John Mark had

* The ones who did not yet believe in Jesus.

quit them once and Paul was afraid he'd do it again. And it's entirely possible that Paul may have been a bit prickly about it too. We don't know for sure.

Barnabas sailed for Cyprus with John Mark.

And Paul took Silas with him and started out on his next missionary journey.

What? I didn't tell you about Silas?

Why, Silas was a very important member of the Jerusalem church—and a Roman citizen, same as Paul. In fact, he was a VIP.*

Anyhow—

It was Paul and Silas from here on. And on this journey with Silas, Paul went farther afield than he had ever been before. To Europe!

They traveled from city to city—until at last they came to Philippi.

And wait till you hear what happened to them in Philippi!!!

* Very Important Person.

12

A MIRACLE THAT SHOOK THE EARTH
Acts 16:12-40

Philippi! Hooray!

And how were things going for Paul and Silas?

A-OK! In fact, today we might say things were going "swimmingly." And to say that things were going swimmingly was putting it very well indeed, for guess where they met to hold their church meetings? Alongside a river!

There they met and there they preached without getting into any trouble—for two whole weeks. And then—

It happened as they were walking toward their "river church" one morning, followed by a friendly crowd.

Suddenly a voice rose high in the air,

"These men are servants of God and they have come to tell you how to have your sins forgiven!"

It was the voice of a young girl.

But there was something strange about it.*

Paul knew at once that something was wrong. And it was. For this poor child was a little slave girl and she was owned by a group of evil men. They had bought her for a very special reason.

She was possessed of an evil demon.**
She could tell fortunes. The evil demon spoke through her. And her owners, the rascals, collected the money!

Paul paid no attention, but just kept on walking, pretending he did not hear. But she cried out again, "These men are servants of God and they have come to tell you how to have your sins forgiven!"

What? A little girl who was possessed with an evil demon could talk about *God*? Yes indeed.*** Paul was *steaming*, but he still said nothing. But when she started to cry it out

* Her voice was high and shrill and she sounded *weird*.
** A spirit of the devil.
*** Even demons believe in God. Just read James 2:19.

again, Paul could stand it no longer. He
stopped in his tracks. And whirled around. He
stared at the girl. And with a voice of
authority—but he did not speak to the girl—he
spoke to the demon in her, "I command you in
the name of Jesus Christ to come out of her!"

Do you know what happened? The wild
look left her eyes—she was perfectly all right
again. The demon had gone!

But her owners? They were FURIOUS!
They knew the jig was up.

They saw all the money they had been
collecting for her fortune-telling go right down
the drain. They turned to those around them
and began to shout against Paul and Silas.
"They are fakers! They have come only to
upset the city!"

And before you could say, "What's going
on?"—Paul and Silas were snatched up and
hauled off to the public square, where the
officials sat in their marble chairs on a raised
platform.

The friendly crowd had become an angry
mob. "These men are upsetting the city!" they
shouted to the officials. "They're teaching

things that are against the Roman law!"

In a moment the verdict came. "Flog them!" and Paul and Silas were tied to the whipping posts—and big brawny Roman soldiers made ready for their horrible task.

Wap! Down came the whips—Wap! Paul and Silas sank to their knees; only the ropes that tied their hands held them up.

After a few more Waps! it was over. And the soldiers dragged them, dazed and fainting, off to a big thick-walled prison, made of stone and with no windows—just huge heavy double doors in front. The soldiers called out to the jailer who came running out from his house alongside.

"Ho," they shouted, "prisoners! These are men who 'show you the way to salvation!' Keep them safe!"

"I'll keep them safe, all right," the jailer muttered. He lifted the heavy bars that bolted the doors. It was dark, dark inside.

Paul and Silas were chained to the walls by their hands, and their feet were locked into wooden frames. The door was closed and bolted—and the footsteps faded away.

It seemed hours before Paul's faintness began to wear off. The pain was becoming worse now—but he was beginning to think clearly.

And he thought, *"If I take the wings of the morning, and dwell in the uttermost parts of the sea, even there shall thy right hand hold me."* * He turned to Silas, and this time he said it aloud.

And there in that stinking prison they lifted their faces and their hearts to God. At first their voices were weak and squeaky, but as they began to praise the Lord their hearts grew lighter and their voices grew stronger and they began to sing!

"God is our refuge and strength, a very present help in trouble; therefore will we not fear.*

The other prisoners stopped their swearing and their groaning. What manner of men were these? Were they crazy? They sounded almost joyful—almost as if they expected some magic—some power to deliver them. Almost as if—

* Read these verses in Psalms 139:9,10; 46:1.

Wait a minute.

What was *THAT*!?!

THUNDER!

No, worse than thunder! The very ground seemed to give way beneath them. The *earth* was *rocking*! The walls of the prison were swaying crazily, threatening to cave in.

Paul and Silas were thrown against each other. Helping each other up they realized that they were free! And their feet! The bolts holding the chains had come loose from the walls. The wooden frames that held their feet were wrenched open! And the cell door was torn from its hinges and sagged outward and crashed to the ground!

A gust of fresh air? Why, the big outer doors had been torn loose also!

By this time the jailer had stumbled his way down from his house. Breathless, he finally arrived at the prison entrance.

He had no light—he couldn't see in—but he could see that the doors had been torn off. There was no sound from inside. That meant only one thing—the prisoners had escaped!

His scalp prickled with fear.

He reached for his short sword, drew it out to kill himself, when—

"Do not harm yourself. We are all here."

It was a voice from inside the prison! The jailer's mind was so bewoggled by this time he could scarcely think. "Over here with the torches," he cried to his assistants who were now struggling down the hill. He grabbed a torch and went inside. And there stood all the prisoners. And in the midst of them stood Paul and Silas. And the words came back to him—*These men show you the way of salvation.*

He was filled with fear. He fell down before them. "Sirs, what must I do to be saved?"

Paul's answer was quick and sure, "Believe on the Lord Jesus Christ, and thou shalt be saved, and thy house."

"My house? My *family*? Sirs—will you tell us—what you mean? I'll take you to my family."

It was a strange procession that filed into the jailer's house where his terrified wife and children were waiting. And there the strangest

church service in the world took place. Paul
told them all about Jesus—how He had died
for them, and how God had raised Him from
the dead. And that they could be saved by
believing that great fact with all their hearts,
and by putting their lives in His hands.

The whole congregation was saved!

The jailer and his wife bathed the wounds
of Paul and Silas. It hurt, but Paul and Silas
hardly felt it, their hearts were so filled with
joy.

And that's not all.

Before the night was over that whole
family was *baptized*—and they all sat down to
eat, Christian friends all together around the
table.*

And that's not all.

Paul and Silas were officially released from
prison. Yes sir, the very next morning the
judges sent police officers over to tell the jailer
to "let those men go!"

But Paul would have none of it.

"Oh, no, they don't," he said. "We are

---

* The other prisoners were probably bathed and fed too. It's
hard to believe that they would have been left out of this
wonderful event.

Roman citizens and now they want us to sneak out of town? Never! Let them come in person and release us and we'll leave town holding our heads up if you please."

So the judges did come in person—right up to the jailer's home—and they *begged* Paul and Silas to leave the city in peace!

And so it all ended happily. Paul and Silas left town all right. But they were not chased out this time.

They *walked* out, holding their heads up!

13

EXTRAORDINARY ADVENTURES OF AN ORDINARY BOY
Acts 21:15—23:31

Do you think Paul and Silas retired and rested for the rest of their lives?

Not so.

They made the same back-breaking journey all over *again*. They went back to all the places they'd already been. And they went to *new places* where they'd never been before.

More and more people became Christians. And miracles happened wherever they went. And people said, "THESE FELLOWS HAVE TURNED THE WORLD UPSIDE DOWN!!!"

And then at last Paul was able to go back to his beloved Jerusalem.

And what happened there? Something very dangerous and exciting—to Paul's *nephew*.

Now Jonathan* was just an ordinary boy who probably spent a lot of his time wishing he could do something adventurous and hair-raising so he could talk about it.

One day he was sitting with his friends just outside the gate leading into the Court of the Gentiles of the Temple. They were swapping yarns of derring-do** when—

"Jonathan!"

"What?" Jonathan swirled around. One of his friends was running towards him.

"Your Uncle Paul is back in Jerusalem. He came on a boat! And some other men with him."

"Oh, boy," Jonathan cried. "My Uncle Paul! I'm going to find him!"

It wasn't until the next day that Jonathan found his uncle.

He was in the court outside the Temple. But something was wrong.

"Men of Israel! Help! This man preaches against our people!" The cries were coming from the Temple. Then the Temple gates were

* The Bible does not tell us what his name was so we're going to give him a name—Jonathan.
** Doing things that are adventurous and hair-raising.

pushed open with a great swoosh, and out came some angry worshipers, dragging a man behind them. Then, of course, the usual thing happened. A mob began to form.

Jonathan stood there frozen with horror. Good grief! The man was Uncle Paul!

Then everything seemed to happen at once. The mob tore at Paul's clothes and beat at him with their fists. The commander of the Roman garrison and his soldiers came flying down the stairs of the Castle of Antonia.* And they plowed into the crowd like a bulldozer.

"Take him to the prison!" the commander shouted to his soldiers. They dragged Paul off through the crowds and towards the steps of the castle. By this time the crowd had become so violent that the soldiers had to hike Paul up on their shoulders so the people wouldn't tear him to pieces.

"Away with him!" they shouted. "AWAY WITH HIMMMM!!!"

"HE'S MY UNCLE PAULLLLL!"

* The Castle of Antonia was high on a rock cliff alongside the Temple and it had towers and apartments and courtyards and baths. But there also were barracks for soldiers and there were prison cells. For the Castle of Antonia was used both as a palace and a prison.

Jonathan shouted. He was almost sobbing by now. He stood there helpless with rage and fighting his tears as he watched them drag Paul up the stairs.

Then suddenly—

Paul turned and said something to the Roman commander and they both stopped, stock still, there on the steps. Jonathan could not hear what was being said. Actually what Paul said to the Roman commander was, "May I have a word with you?" and he said it in perfect cultured Greek. The commander was more than a little surprised; this prisoner sounded like a VIP.*

"I am a Jew," Paul said, "A Jew from Tarsus. And a Roman citizen. I would like to talk to these people for just a moment."

The commander nodded yes and Paul turned towards the crowd and raised his arms for attention. A great silence fell over the crowd. What was going to happen *now*?

"Brothers and fathers," Paul shouted, "listen to me," and he said it in Hebrew which was the language they could best understand

* Very Important Person. Remember?

and they became more quiet than ever.
Jonathan stood there glued to the spot.

"I am a Jew," Paul went on, "born in
Tarsus. But in this city I studied under the
great Gamaliel. And I felt *then* exactly as you
feel *now*. But something happened that
changed my whole life and I want to tell you
about it."

The crowd was quiet, quiet.

And Paul told them how the light from
heaven had blinded him. And how Jesus had
spoken to him. And commanded him to go
preach the gospel—to the Gentiles too.

And when he said *that*, the crowd went
wild again. They tore their clothing. They
threw dust into the air.

And they screamed for his blood!

Jonathan squeezed out of the crowd lest he
be crushed and made for the gate to go home.
The last thing he saw over his shoulder at the
gate was the soldiers carrying Paul up the steps
out of sight and into the castle. There was
nothing to do but wait.

The next morning Jonathan made his way
into the Temple where his class met—and then

suddenly stopped. That group of men he had just passed. He had heard his Uncle Paul's name.

He edged closer to them. And listened.

And what he heard made his scalp prickle underneath his cap. His big adventure had begun. He scuffed his feet on the ground, pretending to look for something. Then he hurried toward the big castle steps, his heart pounding like a trip-hammer! He decided to risk his neck, go see his Uncle Paul, and tell him what he had just heard.

Just getting past the guard was a frightening business. "Please, Sir," Jonathan said. "I—may I please see my uncle? He's Paul, the prisoner who was taken yesterday. It's very important, Sir. It's a matter of life and death."

The guard hesitated just for a moment, and then, "I guess it's all right. Down this corridor. To the right. Here."

And Jonathan followed in silence, until the guard stopped at a cell. Jonathan took hold of the bars. "Uncle Paul!" It was only a whisper, but in a silent corridor it sounded like a shout.

Paul had been pacing the floor, but he stopped and whirled around when he heard Jonathan's voice.

"Jonathan! Jonathan, Son." And he stretched his arms through the bars and took Jonathan by the shoulders to hug him.

"Uncle Paul," Jonathan whispered quickly. "I have heard something. Very important. They are planning to kill you!"

"What do you mean?"

"I was just in the Temple. I overheard them. They have bound themselves by an oath—an oath not to eat or drink until you are dead. They are going to ask the council to send for you again.

"And they'll lie in wait for you and when you are on your way to the council they'll catch you and kill you before you ever get to the council you'll be murdered!" It all came out in one breath.

"You are a very brave lad to come and tell me, Jonathan," Uncle Paul whispered. And then he called out, "Guard!" And then he went on speaking to Jonathan. "The Lord Himself came to me last night and told me not to be

afraid. He promised me that I would go to
Rome. Now, Jonathan, if the Lord said I was
going to Rome, I've got to *live* to get there,
don't I?" he chuckled.

"Oh, Uncle Paul," Jonathan said, "the Lord
Himself?"

Paul didn't answer. The guard had come.

"Guard," he said, "take this boy to the
chief captain. He has something of great
importance to tell him." And he whispered to
Jonathan, "You will not be afraid,
Jonathan!"

"No, Uncle Paul, I won't be afraid."

"Then go with the guard, and the Lord be
with you."

By the time Jonathan reached the captain,
great stabs of fright were shooting up and
down his spine like bolts of lightning. He was
terrified.

"And what is it you want to tell me, Lad?"
the commander said.

And Jonathan started to speak though his
knees had turned to jelly. "Tomorrow," he
said, "the Jews are going to ask you to bring
Paul before the Sanhedrin again and they're

going to pretend that they want to ask a few more questions. But it's not the truth, Sir. For there are more than forty men who are going to be hiding along the road and they plan to jump his guards and then jump *him*—and kill him while he's on his way there. So don't send him, Sir—please don't send him. He will never reach there alive!"

"You're sure this is the truth, Lad?" the commander asked. Then he shouted to one of his assistants. "Make ready 200 soldiers to go to Caesarea!"

"Oh, yes, Sir, it's the truth. I heard it—"

"And horsemen!" the commander called to another assistant. "About seventy of them should do."

He turned again to Jonathan, "And you're his nephew?"

"Yes, Sir. I was on my way to classes when—" but Jonathan never did get a chance to finish.

"Get 200 spearmen!" the captain bellowed again. Then again, back to Jonathan, "Well, you've been a brave lad, Son. You saved me a great deal of trouble. Don't want a prisoner

murdered right under my nose. A Roman
citizen at that." And he thumped his thumbs on
the desk in front of him, and then, "Son? It's
very important that you tell *no* one about this.
For your own safety, Lad."

"No, Sir. I won't tell anyone, Sir."

"Fine," said the captain and then nodded to
Jonathan that he could go.

As Jonathan tiptoed toward the outside
door, he could hear the captain giving orders.
"After it is dark," the captain was saying, "you
will take the prisoner under escort to the
governor at Caesarea. In the meantime I'll
write a letter to the governor—"

That night Jonathan lay on his sleeping mat
long after the family was asleep. Then,
finally—did something he'd never done before.
He dressed quietly, and sneaked past his
parents and let himself out into the street and
disappeared into the shadows.

When he got to the castle he knew where
to go. Around the back, out by the stables—

Ah! there they were! Hundreds of
soldiers—spears shining in the starlight—
horses quietly waiting.

There. There was Uncle Paul. He was wrapped in a cloak with guards on either side. They were helping him up on a horse. Orders were given so quietly Jonathan couldn't even hear them. Then the company started to move. They went right by where he was hiding, squeezed behind bushes, hardly daring to breathe. Uncle Paul rode right by—Jonathan could have reached out and touched him! But instead he waited quietly until the last soldier disappeared into the darkness. Then he started for home, keeping in the shadows.

Little did Jonathan know that he would go down in the greatest history book of all—the Bible—as the nephew of Paul who had overheard the plot to murder him—and who had upset the plans of the murderers!

He only knew, as he let himself back into the house, that this was the greatest adventure of his life.

And the captain had given him orders not to talk about it! Even to his friends!

Or brag about it!

14

THE BIG SHIPWRECK
Acts 27:1-44

It had been three years since that dark, night when Paul was sneaked out of prison and carried off to Caesarea.

They had been three years of nothing but trouble. He had been hauled before governors and kings. The troublemakers of the Sanhedrin in Jerusalem had traveled back and forth, bringing their lawyers with them to complain against him and get him hauled off to court.

But Paul was stubborn. He was, after all, a Roman citizen. He *demanded* to be taken to Rome to be tried. And now, at last, after three years of more trouble than we have room to tell you about—he was on his way! He was at the large and busy port of Myra, a port that harbored vessels from all over the world.

Out of one of the smaller vessels came some soldiers and some men. Not just ordinary men—no. One was Aristarchus and one was Luke, the physician who wrote part of our Bible. And one was Paul. Paul was at last going to go on trial.

They wound their way through the noise and confusion. Julius, the centurion in charge of them, had arranged for them to board a large Alexandrian grain ship bound for Italy. It was part of a famous fleet of ships called "The Breadline of the Roman Empire" that sailed from Egypt to Rome with all kinds of grain. And there it was, waiting for them. It was large—over 180 feet long—with a huge mast and great square sails of flame color. Across its bow they could see the sun shining on the name of the heathen goddess.

The soldiers and prisoners made their way up the gangplank. Julius counted noses, and his prisoners were taken below. And so the big vessel set sail and headed toward Rome with a cargo of wheat and 276 passengers and sailors on board.

They knew it was not going to be an easy voyage. The Mediterranean Sea was sometimes as gentle as a lamb—and sometimes furious and wild.

So they knew it could be dangerous. But little did they know that it was going to be one of the wildest voyages any ship ever made!

The winds were against her from the first. No matter how the captain steered her it was slow going; it was many days before she finally reached the harbor of Fair Havens.

Now by that time it was dangerously close to the time when the winter gales started. From November to March, the sea was declared unsafe. So there was no hope of making it to Rome. They had to find a place to stay for the winter.

"But not here," they argued. "Phoenix is a much better place to stay for the winter, and it should be safe enough; it's only a little way up the coast."

Now Paul was no landlubber. He had traveled all his life as a missionary. And—He knew the Mediterranean Sea in all its moods. "It isn't safe!" he cried. But it was no use.

They all said the same thing—"Nonsense. It isn't as if we were going all the way to Italy. Why, Phoenix is only a few hours away."

And so, in spite of all Paul's warnings, they put out from Fair Havens and headed for Phoenix. And it did look as though they were right. A soft south wind filled the sails. The big boat slid through the lazy blue water as if she were floating on clouds. The lookout, high up on the mast, yawned and stretched and settled down to take a little nap. It surely did look as if Paul, at last, was wrong.

When suddenly—

First the ugly clouds formed over the mountain peaks to the north. And then—

The rest came without warning. The wind came swooping down from the north like a huge GIANT.

It tore at the sails. The ship groaned. And creaked. And shivered in every timber.

Now everybody suddenly came to life and the captain began to shout out frantic orders. "Furl the sails—furl the sails!"

The sailors climbed up the rigging to loosen the ropes and let the big sails down before the wind tore them to pieces.

The men at the rudder-sweeps gave up trying to steer. And the ship just tore loose and leapt through the waters like a frightened animal being chased and not knowing where to go. They had to find shelter soon—for the ship would be torn apart! And then—

"Land ho! Over the bow to windward!" Everyone scurried over to the side of the ship to look. Sure enough—there was an island. They could see it faintly in the distance.

And somehow—*somehow*—the exhausted sailors brought the ship into calmer waters where the island protected them from the wind.

Then came the most dangerous job of all.

They uncoiled huge cables and wrapped them around the hull and across the deck to hold the ship together.

Then with more grunts and groans they set up the stormsail. And slowly and painfully the poor ship limped on her weary way.

The worst of the storm was over now, they hoped. Oh, how they hoped it was over. But it wasn't over. It got worse.

The wind came swooping down again!

It lifted the ship up, up—to the top of huge giant-like waves—and then hurled her down, down, down, again.

And time dragged on. There was no sun. Or moon. Or stars. They could not tell whether it was day or night.

They all gave up hope.

All but Paul.

"Cheer up," he said. "You are not going to die. And I'll tell you why. You're not going to die because I have to be brought to Rome for trial. My life belongs to God. And my job for Him is *not* done yet."

They just stared at him, unbelieving.

"You see," Paul went on, "this very night a messenger of God told me that we would *all* be saved."

Well, they thought he must be crazy. But they did not have to wait long to find out.

For, that very night—

Listen!

Was it?—It couldn't be—but it was! The distant sound of water booming against *land!*

"Land!" they shouted. "Land!"

It was land all right—but the land the water

was dashing against was rocks! Big, jagged,
dangerous rocks! The ship would be hurled
against rocks and torn to pieces!

They slipped down the anchor.

And the ship gro-a-n-ed with a loud
groan—and stopped. But it was tugging and
jerking like a dog trying to get away from his
leash.

Paul waited—and watched. He watched
some sailors move to the bow of the boat.
They were tugging at some ropes.

And then he realized what they were doing.
They were about to lower the lifeboat.
They were going to try to escape to shore in it!

Paul shouted to Julius, "Stop them! Unless
these men stay in the ship here we cannot all
be saved!"

Julius trusted Paul by now and gave quick,
sharp orders. Then some soldiers drew their
swords and cut the ropes. And the lifeboat
pitched down, down, down into the darkness
and disappeared.

Then they waited till morning, holding
their breath. No one dared to sleep.

No one dared to eat, either. Until Paul said

something that made them think that *surely* this time he must be crazy.

"Eat something," Paul said, "for your own good." Then right there in front of them, he bit off a piece of hardtack* and stopped to give thanks to God and began to chew it.

Then slowly, one by one, they dug out their hardtack and began to chew away too. And as they ate, their strength began to slowly come back. And so they waited through the long dark night.

When morning came they realized that all the long days of pitch darkness were gone at last. There was a gray morning light. To their right was a bay. And there was a creek. And a sandy beach. But just ahead of them—rocks, with sharp jagged edges—to tear them apart if they did not swing around in time!

Again the orders shot out, "Hoist the foresail!" And they pulled down the ropes to raise what was left of the tattered sail back up on its mast.

"Cut the anchor cables! Lower the rudders!" The sail filled with wind and billowed out and the

* It was probably something like hard biscuits.

ship began to move. The men at the rudders pulled with all their might to swing the ship around, away from the rocks.

And slowly, slowly—the ship began to swing around—until— She missed the rocks! And headed straight into the bay towards the creek! And then—

The boat began to shiver! She ran aground!

The bow of the ship stuck fast in the sand but the stern was still in the water. And fierce cross-currents grabbed ahold of the tail end of the ship and started to rip it apart as though it was made of paper!

SHE WAS GOING TO SINK!

Now it was every man for himself. And they began to jump overboard. But do you know what those soldiers did? They actually drew their swords and rushed at Paul and the other prisoners—to kill them!*

"No!" yelled Julius. "Let them go! Every man is on his own! Make for the shore the best you can!"

And in one great tangle of men and splintering

---

* The soldiers had been trained to kill prisoners, rather than let them escape.

timber they jumped. And slid.

And fell.

But all of them, one way or another, got pitched into that raging sea.

They disappeared under the water.

And came back up again.

And went down again.

And up again—until one by one they were all hurled onto the sandy beach. And there they lay, still, like a bunch of toy soldiers.

But when they counted noses—WHEN THEY COUNTED NOSES—not one man was missing.

Paul was right. He had trusted God. And God had kept His promise.

15

END OF THE LONG, LONG ROAD
Acts 28:1-31

The shipwrecked sailors and their prisoners did not have any idea where they were. But God knew where they were. They had landed on the island of Malta.*

And there they stayed, for three months, waiting for another ship that would take them on their long trip to Rome.

And did Paul hole up in an inn and rest? And have his meals sent up? He did not. Though he was probably under guard, he went about doing the work God had given him to do, as usual. He told everyone he met all about Jesus. Even the governor and the high officials in the palace.

And by the power of God he healed peo-

* Read the story of their adventures in Malta in Acts 28:1-10.

ple—from the natives to the governor's father!

And when they were finally ready to set sail again, all the people he had told about Jesus—and even the high officials—thanked him. And they loaded him with gifts.

Finally, off they sailed to the great port of Rome itself—Puteoli.*

Paul stood on the deck and gripped the rail and strained his eyes to see ahead. His poor eyesight had gotten worse and worse down through the years and now he was nearly blind. Off to the north were the Roman fleets and the mighty war ships. And dead ahead were the crowded beaches—with the brightly colored sails of the yachts and the ships. Paul could scarcely see them.

And then at last, the gangplank was lowered and Paul and his companions—and his guards—were at last on land again. The goal was in sight, Rome!

The great gateway into Rome. It was called the Porta Capena. And there it stood, sparkling

---

* Don't worry about pronouncing all these names you've been reading. Nobody else can pronounce them either.

in the sun. Many important people had passed through this gate. But this day a man passed through, a thin wiry man—a little stooped now and nearly blind—with many scars on his back underneath his clothing.

Rome did not know it—the man did not look it—but he was one of the most important men in history.

The man was Paul.

Paul, the old warrior now, with many a scar to prove it. And yes, Paul, the bright boy who had fulfilled all his dreams. For he would go down in history as one of the most important men who ever lived. But more than this! For he had also learned patience. And kindness. And love. The things he could never learn from books.

For two years he lived in Rome. And he told the people there "with all boldness about the Kingdom of God and about the Lord Jesus Christ, and no one tried to stop him."

This is the last record we have of Paul. What a man! What a young person he must have been! And what an example he has set for all of us down through the centuries!

DICTIONARY

Agabus. A prophet who lived in New Testament times.

appeal to Rome. If a Roman citizen on trial for a crime felt the trial or verdict was unfair, he could request that the emperor hear the case. Paul, as a Roman citizen, once did this.

Artemis. Greek goddess whose Roman name was Diana. Her most magnificient temple was built in Ephesus.

demon. An evil spirit working for Satan. Christians in the early days were often able to make demons leave a person by the power of Jesus.

Gentile. Any person who is not a Jew.

missionary. Someone who tells others about Jesus. Philip, Peter, Paul, Barnabas, Silas and Timothy were some of the first missionaries.

Pharisee. A member of one of the Jewish religious groups in New Testament times. Pharisees tried very hard to obey every part of the Law Moses gave. At first they sincerely tried to please God and to be holy. Later most of them added many petty rules the religious leaders had made up.

proconsul. The Roman empire was divided into provinces or states. The Roman governor in each province was called the proconsul.

Roman. People born anywhere in the world who were citizens of the Roman Empire. Roman citizens enjoyed special rights and protection. They had to be given a fair trial and could never be crucified.

Sabbath. The seventh day of the week. The Sabbath is the Jewish day of worship and rest.

Sadducee. A member of one of the religious groups which existed in New Testament times. The Sadducees did not believe in a life after death.

Sanhedrin. The highest Jewish political and religious court. In New Testament times the Sanhedrin was made up of 71 experts in Jewish laws. It included the high priest, members of wealthy or prominent Jewish families and members of the Pharisee and Sadducee religious groups.

slave. A person who worked for another without pay. The slave belonged to his or her master. In the Roman Empire, many people were slaves. Often people sold themselves into slavery to pay off their debts. Many wealthy Romans owned large numbers of slaves.

sorcerer. A magician or wizard.

synagogue. A place where people gathered to worship or study. Synagogue services included reading and explaining Old Testament Scriptures and saying prayers.

vow. In New Testament times, when a Jew wanted to thank God in a special way, he or she took a vow which lasted 30 days or longer. While the person was carrying out the vow he or she neither ate meat nor drank wine. Also the person allowed his or her hair to grow.